THE

LAKES DISTILLERY

CUMBRIA

Editor Kathryn Armstrong
Written by Peter Jackson and Ken Oxley
Photography Kevin Gibson, Chris Auld
Design Remember Media

Remember Media Limited
e-volve Business Centre, Cygnet Way,
Rainton Bridge South Business Park, DH4 5QY
www.remembermedia.co.uk

ISBN 978-0-9933710-0-4

FAITH

LOVE

HOPE

LUCK

CONTENTS

CUMBRIAN
SPIRIT

We're not wishing our lives away but December 17, 2017 will be a particularly significant day at The Lakes Distillery.

It will mark three years since the first cask was filled, a day when our precious spirit officially becomes a single malt whisky, in this case, The Lakes Malt.

By then, the near-perfect River Derwent water will have completed its journey, in distance, from its source high up in the hills of Upper Borrowdale at Sprinkling Tarn, and in time, from fermentation and distillation through to the all-important 1,095-day maturation.

In one sense that day will be the end of an amazing journey that has seen The Lakes Distillery rise, quite literally, from the rubble to become a state-of-the-art distilling operation.

With The ONE, we have already created the first British Isles blended whisky as well as our own unique The Lakes Gin and The Lakes Vodka.

Adding The Lakes Malt, 'a drop of liquid gold', to the family will mark the start of another spirited adventure for The Lake Distillery.

Here's the story of the amazing journey so far...

Paul Currie
Founder, The Lakes Distillery

DREAM

Whisky is in Paul Currie's blood. His father set up a distillery on Arran and sowed the seeds for a distillery in the Lake District.

Our story and the history of The Lakes Distillery have their roots in the West of Scotland.

In 1995 Harold Currie and his son Paul set up a distillery on the beautiful Isle of Arran, a brave move as there had been no legal production on the island for almost 160 years and in an industry dominated by the giants it was hard for an independent to survive, let alone start up.

However, Harold was better qualified than most, having been managing director of one such giant, Chivas Brothers. He had long had an affection for Arran and, as a retirement project, he wanted to revive its proud tradition of whisky production.

The early years were indeed a struggle but today Isle of Arran Distillers is thriving. It is one of the island's main visitor attractions and exports its whisky all over the world.

Paul left the business in 2002 to become a drink industry consultant but he never lost a passion for whisky which was reawakened on a holiday with his family to the Lake District in 2010.

He was sure that the area would provide the perfect environment for whisky distilling.

He says: "Dad had the idea of a Lakes distillery even before Arran, so the idea was always in my mind."

It is a drink which is usually associated with Scotland or, as whiskey with an 'e', with Ireland, but there is, in fact, a long tradition of whisky distilling in England.

This tradition died out in the First World War, but with the worldwide growth in interest in whisky and establishment of new independent producers there was a revival and, when Paul had his fateful family holiday there were already five distilleries in other parts of England.

"IT TAKES SEVERAL YEARS TO PRODUCE AND MATURE A SINGLE MALT WHISKY AND THE DISTILLERY HAS STARTED TO LAY DOWN ITS FIRST SINGLE MALT, THE LAKES MALT, WHICH IS DUE FOR BOTTLING IN 2018"

His next task was to identify a suitable site. He enlisted the help of local land agents and explored a number of possible options, a process he recalls that "involved lots of driving around".

In December 2010 in the parish of Setmurthy, near Isel, not far from Cockermouth, he came across a collection of 160-year-old buildings which had originally been a Victorian model farm and had lain empty and derelict for 20 years.

They were in a bad way, but Paul saw that they would make an ideal distillery.

The dream had started to take shape....

"DAD HAD THE IDEA OF A LAKES
DISTILLERY EVEN BEFORE ARRAN,
SO THE IDEA WAS ALWAYS
IN MY MIND. THE PASSION FOR
WHISKY WAS REAWAKENED ON A
HOLIDAY TO THE LAKE DISTRICT.
THE AREA WOULD PROVIDE THE
PERFECT ENVIRONMENT
FOR WHISKY DISTILLING"

PLACE

Forlorn, damp and crumbling the buildings might have been, but the Victorian model farm which is now home to The Lakes Distillery gave Paul Currie a 'Eureka moment' which, after a few hurdles, has been proved right.

P aul Currie discovered the cluster of old farm buildings, nestling under trees, just 150 yards from the River Derwent, and knew he had found what he had been looking for.

The 160-year-old buildings, which had originally been a Victorian model farm, had been left derelict for nearly 20 years.

They were forlorn, damp and crumbling. Exposed to years of unforgiving Lakeland weather, they had suffered extensive water damage which had washed away much of their foundations.

As those foundations had crumbled, walls had settled and were bulging threateningly: nettle and dock were prising their way up through the courtyard and floors and climbing weeds were even beginning to cloak walls.

Even so, it was a case of love at first sight.

"It was a Eureka moment," says Paul Currie.

"We were looking for a site with specific requirements. It had to be big enough to handle all our requirements because, being in the National Park, we couldn't build anything extra; it needed to be accessible and there are plenty of places in the Lakes that are not

accessible; and we needed to be next to a river for a water supply and, preferably, we needed beautiful buildings.

"As soon as I saw the site, all these boxes were ticked. I was very excited."

However, the course of true love never did run smooth and this was to be no exception.

Paul explains: "It did take some imagination because it was a wreck, it was falling apart."

A Carlisle firm of architects, Architects Plus, was engaged and, under the project management of director David Blair, drew up plans for the new distillery.

"I don't think it had any work done on it since it was built originally, so it wasn't in the best of conditions. It needed quite a bit of TLC," recalls David.

However, scraping aside moss and ivy revealed that the original stonework was essentially sound and had been painstakingly worked by the Victorian masons to create some magical features.

Most importantly, the size and layout of the buildings made them ideally suited for conversion into a distillery without the need for extension or embarking on major alteration.

The parish of Setmurthy in which the buildings lay, however, was within the boundaries of the Lake District National Park. Understandably, the park authorities are anxious to preserve the beauty of this unique region and protect it from unsympathetic development.

In seeking to turn the old farm buildings into a distillery therefore, the new enterprise faced some major hurdles.

"Our biggest constraint was the Lake District National Park planning board. We had a lot of discussion back and forth with them, because

"SCRAPING ASIDE MOSS AND IVY REVEALED ORIGINAL STONEWORK THAT HAD BEEN PAINSTAKINGLY WORKED BY VICTORIAN MASONS TO CREATE SOME MAGICAL FEATURES"

essentially they weren't in favour of the development because they classed it as being in the open countryside and would have preferred it in one of the major towns such as Keswick."

Things looked particularly bleak when the planning officer dealing with the application recommended it for refusal.

Paul Currie understood that the officers had to be guided by planning policies but he refused to be deterred. Park planning officials recommended against the plan, but, following a site visit, permission was granted in September 2011 and The Lakes Distillery Company was set up.

Building work started in March 2012, but had to be stopped within a few weeks when the money ran out with just the concrete floor of the still house laid.

However, Architects Plus of Carlisle had announced this in their March newsletter.

It caught the attention and sparked the interest of Nigel Mills. An entrepreneur from the North East, he had been at university in nearby Lancaster from where he explored the Lake District and grew to love the region.

With business interests in the area for some 30 years, he co-owns the Trout Hotel in Cockermouth. He could see the potential for a tourism link with the new distillery.

Paul and Nigel met, agreed to team up and drew up a new business plan as a prelude to launching a concerted fund-raising drive, convincing private investors, public bodies and institutional investors of the viability of their dream.

That summer they teamed up with Dr Alan Rutherford, a leading figure in the Scotch Whisky industry, who introduced them to Chris Anderson, a vastly experienced distiller.

Together with John Bowler, a brewing engineer, they set about designing the best possible distillery plant.

It was vital to get the build moving again.

They then began the process of fundraising, knocking on many doors, giving lots of presentations and even flying potential investors in by helicopter to view the site.

Nigel Mills recalls: "By March 2013 we had raised about £500,000, we had designed our stills and we placed a deposit with McMillans of Edinburgh for the whisky stills and the gin and vodka still."

Then they set about raising the rest of the money seeking it from private investors, and through grants and bank loans. This proved to be a struggle – until they had an inspiration.

"We wondered: what is it we can produce?" says Nigel. "What it is that doesn't exist at the moment? What is it that can demonstrate our expertise, both in terms of blending and in terms of brand development and production?"

"We had this whisky expertise in the business and with that, we thought that if we could produce a product that we could physically show to people it would convince them that we would be capable of building this project. It would also enable us to generate some revenue."

The result was the creation of the first ever British Isles blended whisky, The ONE.

"The ONE was launched in September 2013 at the Taste Cumbria Food Festival and we sold £6,000-worth of whisky over two days from a little wooden bench in the middle of a road in a market town," says Nigel.

This was the catalyst for bringing the project to life because people could see that something tangible was being produced.

"REPLACEMENT MATERIALS HAD TO BE SOURCED FROM WITHIN THE NATIONAL PARK. SLATE COBBLES WERE BROUGHT FROM SOUTH CUMBRIA, SANDSTONE WAS SOURCED FROM NEAR PENRITH. ON THE ROOFS, THE ORIGINAL WESTMORLAND GREEN SLATES WERE CAREFULLY STRIPPED OFF AND REUSED, WHICH WAS THE PRINCIPLE GUIDING THE WHOLE RENOVATION"

From that point a further £3m was raised and work on the distillery began again in April 2014.

The distillery team looks back with gratitude to Architects Plus and builders Lambert Gill Construction who had still been owed money from the first and short-lived phase of the building but who had kept faith with the project.

"Architects Plus waited over a year for us and Lambert Gill waited nearly two years for their money," says Nigel. "We rewarded them because their original contract was £1m and as it turned out the conversion of the buildings was £2.5m. It was a great example of local tradesmen trusting people who were going to build something locally and that was at a time when money was really tight for everybody. We rewarded loyalty with loyalty."

Once funds were promised, builders could again start work. This they did in the early spring of 2014, all too aware that they were facing a tight deadline.

Under the terms of the lease, work had to be completed by the end of the year but this was a challenging project and the nature of the site and its access roads meant it could not be flooded with labour and machinery.

"It was a major exercise because we were virtually rebuilding a lot of the buildings," says David Blair. "We had to do a lot of very careful underpinning work, replacing floors. It was quite a restricted site as well so you couldn't hit it with hundreds of people. There was a sequence in which it all had to be carried out which was quite complex."

There were to be many complications, foreseen and unforeseen.

Just off the main production building stood a more modern single-storey structure with an asbestos cement roof which had to be carefully stripped off and disposed of.

This was replaced with a colour-coated metal to give a more agricultural look in keeping with the rest of the complex.

The building which now houses the bistro demanded extensive and complex work.

David Blair explains: "The more that we started stripping back, the

"THE UNIQUE, SPECIALLY DESIGNED LAKES DISTILLERY STILLS WERE DELIVERED IN JUNE 2014 AND WERE COMMISSIONED IN DECEMBER 2014. DECEMBER 16TH WAS A MOMENTOUS DAY, THE FIRST DAY THAT SPIRIT FLOWED"

worse we found it was. The front wall of that building had an alarming bulge in it, due to the amount of rain water and flooding working away at the foundations.

"The wall had a bow at the top, so that at eaves level it was about 12" out of plumb, and it was leaning outwards like the Leaning Tower of Pisa, so we had to look at some interesting engineering solutions to stabilise that. In the end, it was in such bad condition that we actually ended up having to rebuild quite a significant portion of the front wall, to make it structurally sound."

To make matters worse, the floors of the building – which had only served as a cow byre in its previous life – were not level, with an 18" difference from one end to the other.

The architects contemplated steps to handle the gradient but that would have created problems for disabled access, so the foundations had to be underpinned before the floor could be stabilised and levelled. Above that, the whole roof structure had to be replaced with matching replacement king post trusses, which are now on view inside the building.

A smaller single-storey building which now houses the shop and reception had also formerly been a cow byre.

"It had timber roof trusses, with cast iron metal posts, which again had quite an alarming lean on them," says David Blair. "We had to get approval to take that down and basically rebuild that building, which we have done."

All the stones were numbered and carefully replaced in their original positions, with the important difference that the wall they formed was no longer leaning. Again the roof had to be replaced and new royal post trusses fitted supported with new steel work to match the old.

Outside, the courtyard was originally a mixture of concrete and earth. It also had a fall of about 18" from end to end, presenting a challenge in creating the present outdoor seating area.

The Lake District planning board insisted that all replacement materials had to be sourced from within the national park, so for the courtyard, slate cobbles were brought from South Cumbria. Where new sandstone was needed it was sourced from near Penrith. For the roofs, the original Westmorland green slates were carefully stripped off and reused where possible, which was the principle guiding the whole renovation.

David Blair explains: "We reused 80% of the original stone. Anything that was taken down and could be put back again was put back again. In the bistro wing, where we had to rebuild part of the existing wall, any stone and all of the existing lintels were numbered, photographed and put back into the same position. Essentially, there was nothing thrown away, everything that was taken down was reused where it could be.

"There was a requirement for some new stone but that was mainly to the retaining walls to the car park. We were able to reuse any internal walls that came out."

For Paul Currie it was a long and sometimes tortuous journey to realising his distillery dream.

And, as for any true lover of the Lakes, there is always another mountain to climb.

As he says: "This project was four years in the making and to have the whole thing come to fruition was a big moment.

"But this is only the beginning of the story, we have now got to build a great company and a great brand around the globe."

"I never doubted that we would get this through because the logic of what we were trying to do and how it would benefit the local community and preserve these wonderful old buildings would be sufficient to get it through."

"BRITISHNESS, AN ISLAND NATION AND TOGETHERNESS. ONE IDEA STOOD OUT LIKE A SORE THUMB BECAUSE THIS WAS THE ONLY BRITISH WHISKY, AND THAT WAS TO CALL IT, THE ONE"

COFFEE
NOW
BEING
SERVED

QUATREFOIL

While renovating the structure, the builders uncovered many beautiful original details in the architecture and stonework which the architects were careful to incorporate into the new building. Foremost among these was a recurring quatrefoil motif.
The quatrefoil is an ancient Celtic Christian symbol which denotes Faith, Hope, Luck and Love.
It has become a key symbol of The Lakes Distillery, underlining the very qualities which made this remarkable building possible.

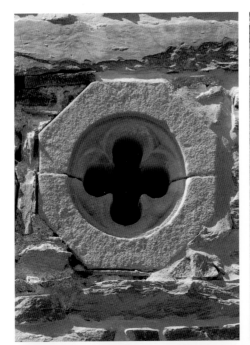

41

LAND

Land and the water create fine flavours, think of the famous wine growing regions of France. Few things are associated as closely with location as whisky, a drink which is the very essence of the soil and stream.

Place is an essential part of any great drink, arguably, it is its most important single ingredient.

The land and the water create great tastes, whether in the famous wine growing regions of France or in the Highlands of Scotland. And nothing is associated as closely with location as whisky, a drink which is the very essence of the soil and streams that are so fundamental to its creation.

It is no accident then that the people who first conceived the idea of The Lakes Distillery saw in the Lake District the ideal place in which to create their whisky.

"The Lake District has been a central part of my life, I've been there a lot from a young age," says Lakes Distillery founder, Paul Currie. "It's just so different from the rest of England, an oasis of greenery and mountains and lakes, it's just fantastic."

Renowned for its beauty, the Lake District was one of the last great Celtic strongholds of England and had its own tradition of whisky

"DERWENT IS CELTIC FOR RIVER OF OAKS. WATER AND OAK, WHICH MAKES THE BARRELS IN WHICH THE SPIRIT IS MATURED, ARE TWO OF THE KEY INGREDIENTS OF WHISKY"

"RENOWNED FOR ITS BEAUTY, THE LAKES WAS ONE OF THE LAST GREAT CELTIC STRONGHOLDS WITH ITS OWN TRADITION OF WHISKY DISTILLING. WITH ITS WILD PEATY FELLS AND PURE WATER TUMBLING OFF THEM DOWN HIDDEN VALLEYS THE LAKES IS MADE FOR WHISKY"

distilling. Little wonder, for it can be a hard land to those who work it. A place where a warming spirit is welcome.

With its wild, peaty fells and pure water tumbling off them down hidden valleys, the Lakes is made for whisky.

It is a land of contrasts: of louring windswept moorland and placid, shimmering lakes; a land where black, threatening clouds are broken by sudden shafts of golden sunlight; of silence broken only by the cry of the solitary curlew which can then be filled with the clamour of a hundred chuckling streams or the angry crashing of a waterfall.

The land has been forged by nature and man.

Its mountains were created some 50 million years ago from some of the oldest rocks in the world and since then they have weathered evenly to produce the characteristic smooth-sided, softly rounded mountains, but there are still plenty of sharp-edged crags and cliffs towering over vast sheets of water gouged out by the relentless glaciers.

It has been inhabited from the earliest times by peoples who made their mark with mysterious stone circles, to be followed by the Romans with their more practical forts and roads.

Norsemen built farmsteads and cleared the thickly wooded fells for grazing and, along with the Celts, bequeathed the evocative place names.

The land continued to be marked by the spoil of quarryman and miner and the trod of shepherd.

This unique landscape was loved and lauded by the poets who have made it known throughout the world and revered even by those who have never seen it.

Most famous of these bards was, of course, Wordsworth who wrote of this "little, unsuspected paradise".

"THE DERWENT'S PURE WATER AND THE LAND THROUGH WHICH IT FLOWS GIVE THE DISTILLERY'S PRODUCTS THEIR DISTINCTIVE CHARACTER AND UNIQUE TASTE"

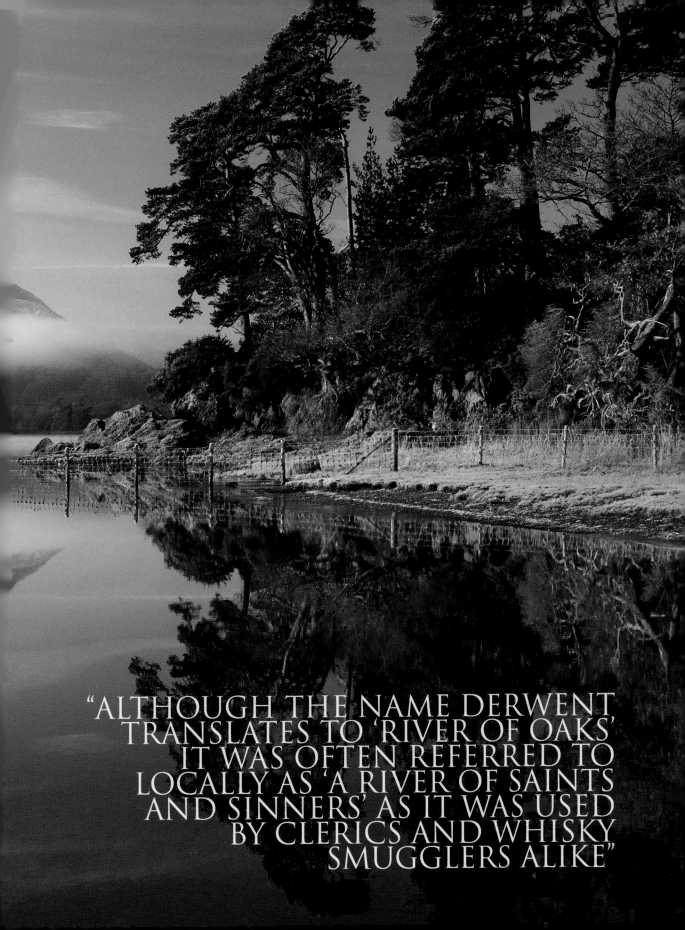

"ALTHOUGH THE NAME DERWENT TRANSLATES TO 'RIVER OF OAKS' IT WAS OFTEN REFERRED TO LOCALLY AS 'A RIVER OF SAINTS AND SINNERS' AS IT WAS USED BY CLERICS AND WHISKY SMUGGLERS ALIKE"

WELCOME

A visitor to The Lakes Distillery will be struck by the magnificent gates which guard the entrance.

It is traditional for breweries and distilleries to have a grand and distinctive entrance to reflect the stature of the brand which lies behind them both metaphorically and literally.

The Lakes Distillery's Nigel Mills had this in mind when he went on a family holiday to California in the summer of 2014 and, while in the Napa Valley, saw that some of the vineyards boasted ornate gates.

He was also inspired by the Queen Elizabeth Gate at Hyde Park Corner in London, made to celebrate the 90th birthday of the late Queen Mother.

"I decided we needed something like that, something to make a real statement before you even get into the distillery so that they reflect the prestige quality and excellence that we are pursuing in everything that we do.

"I said to the architects, we need to find some international artist of renown who can create this vision."

They commissioned the creative design agency Hedley McEwan to

create a video of what the gates should look like to reflect The Lakes Distillery's logo with barley, juniper and other botanicals that go into the spirits and, of course, the quatrefoil.

Architects Plus undertook a search for a suitable artist and found Alan Dawson, a man who has worked in art and architectural metalwork for more than 35 years.

He has produced acclaimed works in Abu Dhabi, Dubai and London and not only that but his company Adaptahaus is based in Maryport in Cumbria.

They met him, discussed the project with him and then commissioned him to create the gates to be made from galvanised iron which have been powder-coated and then hand-painted.

Nigel says: "We let him get on with it and he turned up in December with these gates and we thought, my goodness, they are amazing and they are the embodiment of all aspects of what we have produced."

ROOTS

The magic of the distilling process spans the centuries with a fascinating history that takes in saints, sinners and smugglers.

W hisky has a long and mysterious history. There is evidence of distilling in Syria as far back as 800AD using the grain 'bere'.

And legend has it that St Patrick introduced distilling in Ireland in the fifth century.

However, the first written account of whisky distillation anywhere in the United Kingdom was in Scotland in 1494 by Friar Jon Cor.

At an ancient abbey in Fife, on the banks of the Tay, Cor, a Tironensian monk, paid duty of "eight Bols of malt wherewith to make Aqua Vitae for King James IV" – enough, apparently, for 1,500 bottles of whisky. This reference in the Exchequer Rolls is the earliest documented record of distilling in Scotland.

By the late 17th century ever-increasing taxation rates on alcohol had given rise to an army of illicit distillers who hid their equipment high in the hills to escape the watchful eyes of Excise men.

And whilst The Lakes Distillery prides itself on being the first to produce legal whisky here, the region had no shortage of moonshiners and smugglers.

Indeed, although the name Derwent translates to 'river of oaks' it was often referred to locally as 'a river of saints and sinners' as it was used by clerics and whisky smugglers alike.

The most notorious moonshiner by far was Lancelot 'Lanty' Slee, who was born around 1800 in Borrowdale and lived at Low Arnside between Skelwith Bridge and Coniston.

Lanty – described in records as 'a stiff fresh-faced man of great endurance' – had stills hidden all over the Cumbrian hills, and even in caves.

He had many regular customers, including a local magistrate. However, HMC did finally catch up with him in 1853, fining him the then astronomical sum of £150 (about £18,000 in today's money).

It wasn't long, however, before he was back in business, finding new out-of-the-way locations for his illicit stills. Lanty was known to be making his potent spirit well into his 60s and lived to the grand old age of 78, quite an achievement given the much lower life expectancy of the time. Perhaps the Aqua Vitae – literally, 'water of life' – played a part in his longevity.

Despite his unsavoury past – or perhaps because of it – Lanty has become a star attraction at The Lakes Distillery, making a special 'guest appearance' at the visitor centre to relay his story.

SOURCE

From its source at the magically-named Sprinkling Tarn, the River Derwent runs to the sea through a wealth of history. Its pure water and the land through which it flows give The Lakes Distillery's products a distinctive character and unique taste.

The River Derwent rises 2,500ft up in the hills of Upper Borrowdale, high on the northern flank of Scafell Pike, then tumbling down the fells to feed two lakes before winding through gentle meadows to the Irish Sea. Derwent is Celtic for River of Oaks; and water and oak – which makes the barrels in which the spirit is matured – are two of the key ingredients of whisky.

The Derwent, which rises in Sprinkling Tarn is a spate river and is one of the fastest flowing in Europe. This, combined with the unspoilt and heavily protected land through which it flows makes it exceptionally pure with a turbidity of just 0.5 on a scale of 1 to 100+.

The Derwent is so important to the business that the Lakes Distillery chartered a helicopter equipped with a £1.2m high definition camera, and the same crew that shot David Attenborough's Life on Earth series and the BBC documentary Coast, to film the river's journey from its source to the sea.

The film, which is now a central feature of the distillery tour, begins at Sprinkling Tarn in Upper Borrowdale and then follows the stream, swooping down through the spectacular scenery to Derwentwater. In the centre of the lake sits St Herbert's Island, home of the saint until his death in 687AD.

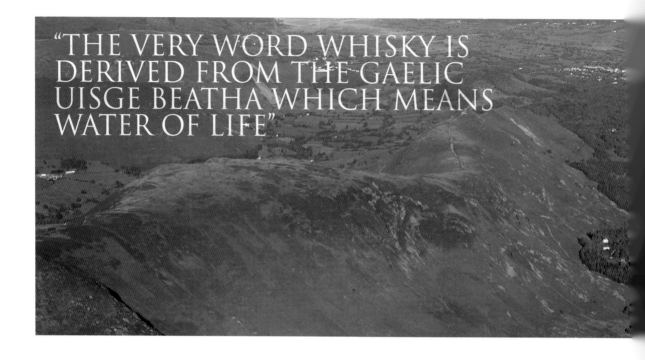

"THE VERY WORD WHISKY IS DERIVED FROM THE GAELIC UISGE BEATHA WHICH MEANS WATER OF LIFE"

The Derwent is sometimes called the River of Saints and Sinners, for, apart from St Herbert, it was used by smugglers who transported their contraband along it in 'kats', broad beamed and shallow drafted boats.

Derwentwater ends at Keswick, where the river flows out of the lake to wander through a marshy low lying area before entering Bassenthwaite Lake. This, strictly speaking, is the only true lake in the Lake District, the others being 'meres' or 'waters'.

At about four miles, Bassenthwaite is one of the longest bodies of water in the Lake District.

The River Derwent flows out of the northern end of the lake and then turns west to pass The Lakes Distillery. Shortly afterwards it passes Isel's St Michael's Church, which dates from 1130 and neighbouring Isel Hall, a charming patchwork of Tudor and Jacobean architecture.

The river then snakes its way to Cockermouth where it is joined by the River Cocker, their confluence overseen by the ruins of Cockermouth Castle, which sits on a mound above the rivers.

Cockermouth's most famous son is the poet William Wordsworth who was born there in 1770 and who went to school with Fletcher Christian of HMS Bounty fame.

The Derwent has always been famed for its salmon fishing and at Salmon Hall remains

of fish traps can still be found in the river.

Finally, as the river reaches the sea at Workington, there are reminders of its history on all sides. The Romans were here, as were the Vikings and Mary Queen of Scots.

Workington's Barepot Ironworks made some of the cannon and cannon balls that secured victory at Trafalgar and also components for Stephenson's Rocket.

In such a short distance the Derwent covers varied and beautiful scenery and spans a wealth of history. Its pure water and the land through which it flows give the distillery's products their distinctive character and unique taste.

The film captures the mercurial beauty of the river, as Duncan McEwan from creative design agency Hedley McEwan explains.

"When we're up near Sprinkling Tarn, we're actually sat under the low lying cloud which didn't even clear Scafell. We're sort of sat under the cloud, and it had a real brooding feel to it, but, as we came down the valley, over Derwent Water and over Bassenthwaite, passing the distillery and over towards the sea, it just got brighter and brighter and brighter, and then by the time we got to the sea, it was like the Mediterranean.

"It's all to do with the landscape in which The Lakes Distillery sits, it's just a great story and a great location."

MASH

The principles of whisky distillation have changed little since the days of Lanty and the smugglers.
Today the difference is the use of technology and more sophisticated equipment to make the most of those three magic ingredients, malted barley, yeast and water. Years of experience and knowledge also helps, of course.

There are five stages to the process: malting, mashing, fermentation, distillation and maturation.

MALTING

Barley contains starch which needs to be converted into soluble sugars to make alcohol. This happens when the barley undergoes the process of germination, also known as 'malting'. Dry barley seeds are steeped in water over two or three days before being spread on the floor of a malting house, the more traditional method, or placed in large, slowly rotating, drums to germinate. When this occurs, after four to five days, the barley is kiln dried which halts germination. It is then ground down in a mill at the distillery to produce grist. The Lakes Distillery sources its malted barley from nearby North Yorkshire as Cumbrian barley

does not have a sufficiently high enough starch content for whisky distillation.

MASHING

The milled barley, or 'grist' as it is now called, is mixed with warm water, and this is referred to as the 'mash'. It is fed into a large, circular vessel called a 'mash tun' where it is stirred for several hours. The mashing process is the means by which the starches in the barley convert to sugars, which will later be fermented into alcohol. As the sugars dissolve, they are drawn off through the bottom of the mash tun, and the resulting liquid is called 'wort'. Once the process is complete, any residue such as husks is called 'draff'. This is not wasted, but collected and used in the production of animal feed.

FERMENTATION

The wort is cooled and passed into large tanks called 'washbacks'. Here the yeast is added to begin the fermentation process. The yeast turns the sugars that are present into alcohol. At The Lakes Distillery, this normally takes about 90 hours. At this point the liquid is called 'wash' and is low in alcohol, approximately 8%, like a strong beer. Indeed, you could make beer from the wash – the difference is that the liquid is now distilled rather than brewed.

DISTILLATION

Copper has been found to be the best material for extracting impurities from spirit as it is being distilled. The stills are essentially giant kettles with a bowl shape at the bottom that rises up to the neck at the top.
All are broadly the same although different shapes will change the flavour and character of the final spirit. The Lakes Distillery's stills have been designed with a particular character of spirit in mind.
The stills work in pairs.
Firstly the wash enters the large still, or wash still, and is heated.
The liquid vaporises and rises until it reaches the neck and then

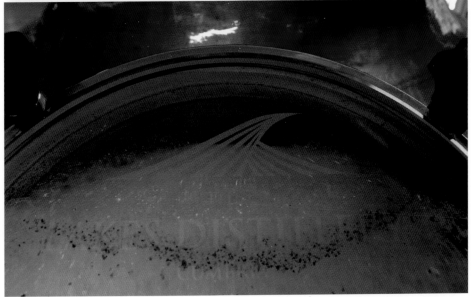

♣ 16th December 2014 – The first spirit flows

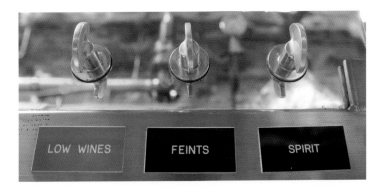

passes into the condenser. This liquid is called 'low wines' and has an alcohol level of 22% to 24%.

These low wines are then passed into a second, smaller still – known as the spirit still – where the alcohol is split into three constituent parts – foreshots, the middle cut, and feints.

Foreshots are high in alcohol but, because of the levels of impurities they contain, they are unsuitable to be kept for maturation. Only alcohol from the middle cut, or 'heart', of the distillation process is used.

This is normally just 20% of the spirit with a strength of 65-70% alcohol by volume (ABV) and is skilfully removed and collected by the 'stillman'. The feints, alcohol from the end of the process, are weak and also unsuitable for maturation. However, neither the foreshots nor the feints get wasted, they are mixed with the next batch of low wines and re-distilled.

MATURATION

The spirit is put into oak casks and stored. The Lakes Distillery uses a variety of casks, some of which have been previously used to store sherry, others bourbon. During maturation, the flavours of the spirit combine with the natural compounds of the wood to give the whisky its unique characteristic flavour and aroma. However, it does not become whisky until it has spent at least three years in its cask, before this it is mere spirit.

HOW WE MAKE
THE LAKES SINGLE MALT

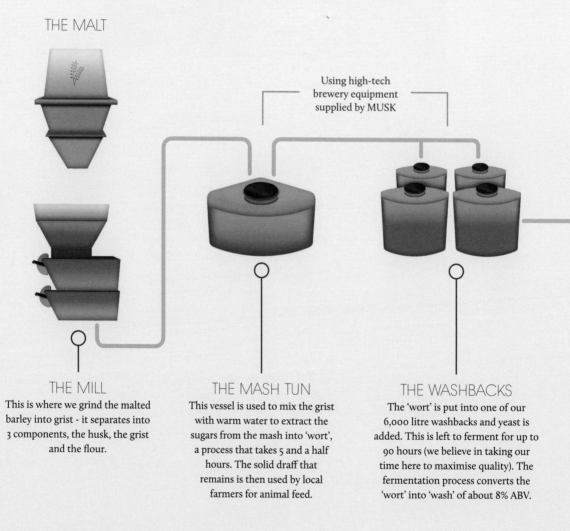

THE MALT

Using high-tech
brewery equipment
supplied by MUSK

THE MILL

This is where we grind the malted barley into grist - it separates into 3 components, the husk, the grist and the flour.

THE MASH TUN

This vessel is used to mix the grist with warm water to extract the sugars from the mash into 'wort', a process that takes 5 and a half hours. The solid draff that remains is then used by local farmers for animal feed.

THE WASHBACKS

The 'wort' is put into one of our 6,000 litre washbacks and yeast is added. This is left to ferment for up to 90 hours (we believe in taking our time here to maximise quality). The fermentation process converts the 'wort' into 'wash' of about 8% ABV.

THE WASH STILL

The first distilling point where our 5000 litre wash still drives off alcohols, which are collected by the still man at pre-determined cut points to result in a spirit of 20% ABV. The remaining 'Low Wines' is used in the next distillation stage.

CONDENSERS

We use both copper and stainless steel condensers to cool the distillate back into liquid before it heads to the spirit still. We are the first distillery to use these two types of condenser, which help to give a greater character to our spirit.

After the spirit moves through the spirit still it flows back through a second set of condensers before heading to the spirit safe.

SPIRIT STILL

This is the second distillation stage using our 3500 litre spirit still. The resulting spirit 'cut' from this process produces a new make spirit of around 70% ABV.

Traditional stills and condensers from McMillan (Scotland)

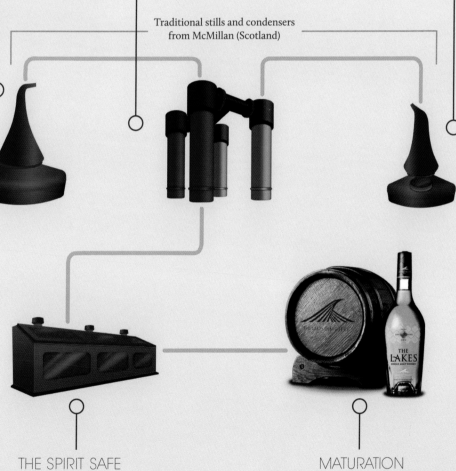

THE SPIRIT SAFE

This is a tool used by the Stillman to observe the strengths of the distillation and to make the cut of new make spirit that will mature into The Lakes Malt.

MATURATION

The final step in production, but arguably the most important, is the transfer of our spirit into high quality wooden casks. Here we let the spirit sleep to allow the wood to work its magic, as our spirit matures into a wonderful single malt.

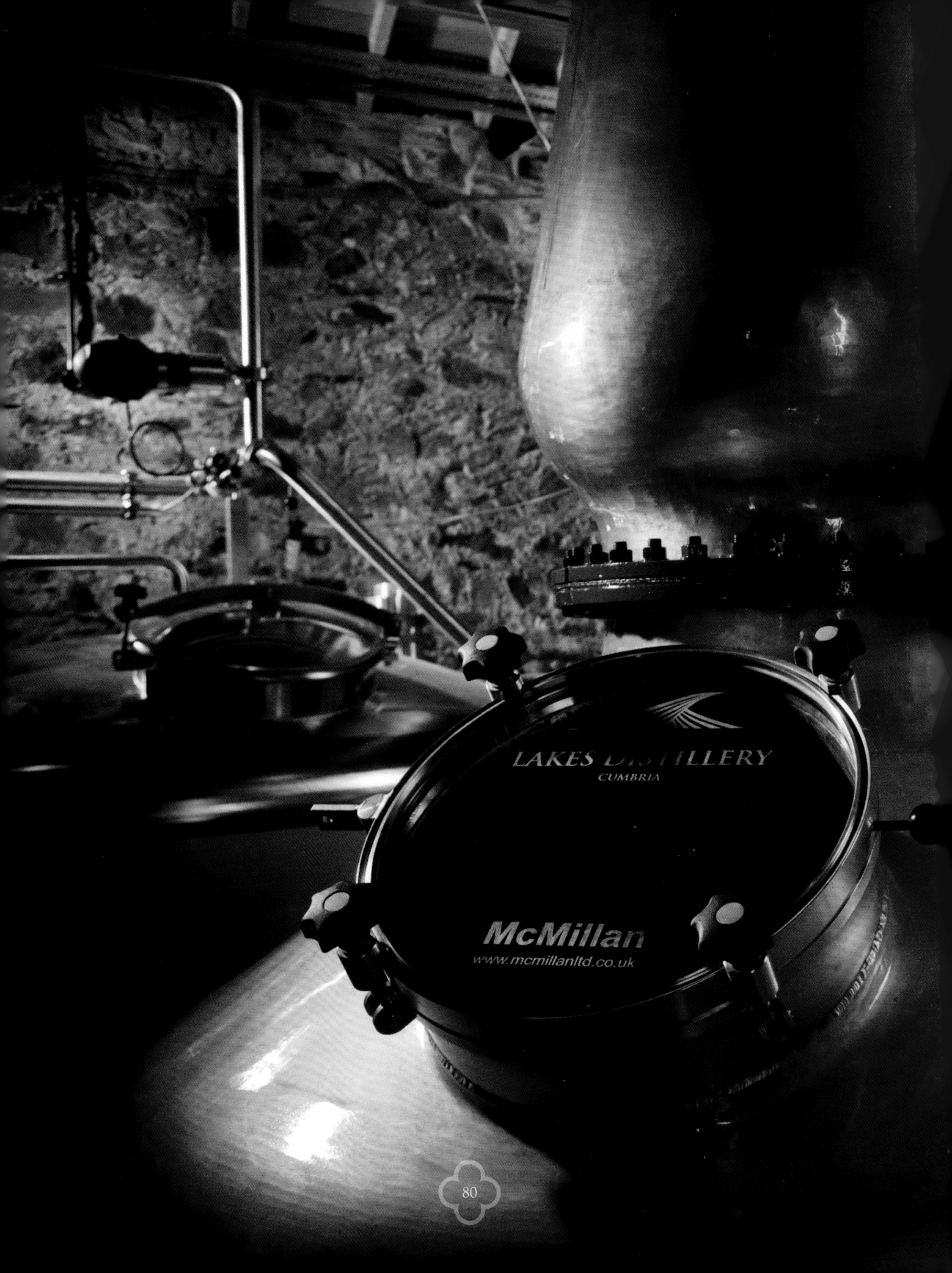
LAKES DISTILLERY
CUMBRIA
McMillan
www.mcmillanltd.co.uk

STILL

The gleaming whisky still is a place where science and nature combine to work their malty magic.

In the beating heart of The Lakes Distillery, gleaming copper stills reach gracefully to the ceiling like abstract sculptures. It's impossible not to be seduced by the beauty of these giant, bulbous creations or impressed by the complex series of pipes, twitching needles and misty portholes that tease visitors with a glimpse of the contents within.

This is the engine room of the operation, a state-of-the-art and laboratory-clean place where centuries of tradition have been finely-honed. And yet, all of this technology is devoted to just three humble ingredients – malted barley, yeast and water.

What is perhaps even more remarkable is that these ingredients, depending on how they are distilled and matured, are capable of producing a seemingly endless variety of whisky styles, from heavy, peaty drinks that deliver a full-blown assault on the senses to those that are delicate, sweet and floral.

With this in mind, creating a whisky that stands out from the crowd is a formidable challenge. The Lakes Distillery Managing Director Paul Currie and Chairman Nigel Mills are confident they have something rather special maturing in the distillery's oak casks.

The eagerly-awaited The Lakes Malt must remain in those casks, previously used for sherry and bourbon, for a minimum of three years. Then, and only then, can it be officially classed as whisky. But the wait will surely be worthwhile. For whilst the distillation stage of the process is all about chemistry – creating the alcohol and removing impurities – the maturation stage delivers the real magic as the spirit slowly draws character and colour from the natural wood.

Few people understand this process better than Dr Alan Rutherford OBE, Director of The Lakes Distillery, who is widely acknowledged as one of the world's leading whisky experts. His career spans almost 40 years. He is a former Council Member of the Scotch Whisky Association and was Scotch Whisky Production Director at United

RACHEL

CHEMMY

THE
LAKES DISTILLERY
CUMBRIA

McMillan
www.mcmillanltd.co.uk

Distillers, later Diageo. So what, in his view, does it take to create a world-class single malt?

Before it goes into the still, the fermented liquor contains heavy, sulphur-bearing compounds, the most common of which are mercaptans.

Although harmless, mercaptans have a pungent smell, often described as similar to rotting cabbages. However, as the vapours inside the still condense onto the copper surface, the resulting chemical reaction causes these compounds to be removed.

Alan explains: "Copper plays an extremely important part in the

"IT'S IMPOSSIBLE NOT TO BE SEDUCED BY THE BEAUTY OF THESE GIANT, BULBOUS CREATIONS OR IMPRESSED BY THE COMPLEX SERIES OF PIPES, TWITCHING NEEDLES AND MISTY PORTHOLES THAT TEASE VISITORS WITH A GLIMPSE OF THE CONTENTS WITHIN"

chemistry of distillation by removing the mercaptans. That's why it's by far the best material to use. If you distilled in glass and steel, you'd make a pretty grim whisky... it just wouldn't be drinkable."

The copper also dissolves, in minute quantities, into the spirit, and the more copper you have in your spirit, the lighter it becomes. This, explains Alan, is why small stills, where the copper-to-liquid ratio is greater, produce light whiskies whilst large stills produce heavier ones.

So does this mean The Lakes Distillery, with its relatively small stills, is destined to produce a light, delicate malt? The answer is yes... and no. The distillery team worked closely with engineering company Musk, who provided the mash tun and wash backs, and leading coppersmiths McMillan to design stills that have a number of ground-breaking features.

One unique touch is the incorporation of nautical-style portholes that allow workers to see what's going on inside. And it comes as no surprise to learn this feature is also extremely popular with visitors who take part in the distillery tour. Playing a key role at this early stage was brewery consultant John Bowler, of J M Bowler Ltd, who, together with Peter Laws, former Head Brewer with Jennings in Cockermouth, helped bring Alan Rutherford's vision to life. Another specialised aspect of the design, and one which has a greater impact on the production process, is the inclusion of stainless steel condensers in addition to the traditional copper variety.

"OUR FIRST SINGLE MALT WILL BE A LIGHT ONE, AND THAT'S FINE BECAUSE THAT'S WHAT WE ARE AIMING FOR. WE'RE LOOKING TO PRODUCE A LIGHT, SWEET MALT WITH A CHARACTERISTIC OF ITS OWN THAT MAKES IT A UNIQUELY LAKELAND DRINK – NOTHING TOO FIERCE OR HEAVY"

Alan explains: "Our first single malt will be a light one, and that's fine because that's what we are aiming for. We're looking to produce a light, sweet malt with a characteristic of its own that makes it a uniquely Lakeland drink – nothing too fierce or heavy. I want it to be a whisky anyone would be proud to serve and I've no doubt it will be.

"But what makes our set-up here special, is that we're not limited to producing light malts. Because our stills have been specially designed to include the stainless steel condensers, we can exercise some control over the amount of copper contact on the liquid. This gives us a lot of flexibility to experiment and the ability to produce a heavier whisky if we want to."

THE LAKES DISTILLERY

CUMBRIA

Great care and skill is needed throughout the whisky making process, from the malting of the barley to mashing and fermenting before distillation and, finally, the maturation stages. But even with a highly skilled team and the finest equipment money can buy, the finished article remains beholden to nature. Because without an abundant supply of high quality water, the resulting whisky is destined to disappoint. Fortunately for The Lakes Distillery, it could not have wished for a more pure, or reliable, source. Its supply is drawn from the River Derwent, just 150 yards away from the building. It begins its journey high up in the hills of Upper Borrowdale at Sprinkling Tarn, just below Scafell Pike. From here it speeds its way through peaty foothills and then into, and out of, Bassenthwaite Lake before meeting the sea at Workington, some 25 miles away. And 'speed' it does. As a 'spate river' flowing through a region reputed to have the highest levels of rainfall in England, the Derwent is one of the fastest flowing rivers in Europe. These environmental factors clearly have an influence on the water that finds its way into The Lakes Malt. Indeed, the results from a sample sent to a leading analytical chemist to the whisky industry confirmed its purity.

The report stated the water is of an ideal PH level and is very soft – both important qualities for water in whisky production. Another key factor is its 'turbidity', which is a measure of the water's clarity. On a scale of 0 to over 100, with 0 being perfection, the distillery's water scored 0.6 – and a more recent test recorded 0.45, which is exceptional.

"ONE UNIQUE TOUCH IS THE INCORPORATION OF NAUTICAL-STYLE PORTHOLES THAT ALLOW WORKERS TO SEE WHAT'S GOING ON INSIDE"

CASK

The influence of wood on the whisky spirit cannot be overstated, it has a huge effect.

At the beginning of the maturation process, the liquid is virtually clear. Over time, however, it picks up colour and flavour from the wood in which it gently steeps, finally taking on the golden hues we know and love.

Sherry casks, made with European oak, impart flavours such as sultanas, raisins, candied peel, cinnamon, nutmeg and caramel. By contrast, bourbon casks, made with American oak, produce flavours such as vanilla, honey, coconut, almonds, fudge and ginger. It's crucial to have top quality casks. And it was here that Alan Rutherford's knowledge and contacts proved invaluable for a fledgling distillery.

"Obviously I know a lot of people in the whisky industry so getting hold of quality casks was not as difficult as you might imagine," he says, "especially as we weren't looking for high volumes.

"Coopers, whether they're in Scotland, America or Portugal, are always interested in new distilleries – and I found they took a particular interest when I told them we were based in the Lake District."

Alan sourced high-quality bourbon and sherry casks made from oak which will be used for the bulk of the operation. However, one of the advantages of setting up a distillery south of the border is that it affords options not open to Scottish producers.

"Strict guidelines mean that Scottish whisky must be matured in oak," says Alan. "However, we are not bound by those rules in England. We do still have to adhere to European regulations so, for example, our spirit must still be matured in wood for three years before we can call it whisky. But the good news for customers is that we have the freedom to experiment with different types of wood.

"So whilst the vast majority of our whisky will come from oak, we will perhaps try using maple or chestnut. The idea is to have a 'Mad March' – just one month of the year when we try something a bit different."

The
Lakes Distillery Company

2015
100

FOUNDERS
145·3

INSPIRE

Those aesthetically pleasing copper whisky stills are named in time-honoured tradition, after women. The wash still is Susan, after Chairman Nigel Mills' wife, whilst the spirit still is Rachel, after MD Paul Currie's wife. The preference for copper has nothing to do with the fact that its hues are reflected in the resulting spirit when it emerges from wood, as romantic a notion as that might seem. It is entirely down to science.

SUSAN

CONDENSERS

RACHEL

UNION

The creation of a first-ever blend of whiskies from the British Isles was a lightbulb moment for The Lakes Distillery team, flicking the switch of success from the stills.

I n the spring of 2013, as the groundswell of support for a referendum on Scottish independence gained momentum, the coalition government sought to counter the claims of the 'yes' camp by launching its 'Better Together' campaign.

And, somewhat surprisingly, these political machinations north of the border became an unlikely source of inspiration for The Lakes Distillery team.

The planned single malt would not be ready for bottling for another four years at least, and it was felt the distillery needed to make its presence felt before then.

It was decided that a statement of intent was called for in the form of a blended whisky bearing the distillery's name.

A pure English blend was out of the question.

Dr Alan Rutherford explains: "There simply weren't enough English whiskies to make such a blend viable.

"As we were weighing up various options, the 'Better Together' campaign was just getting started and I think it was Paul who first

suggested the idea of a British Isles blend using whiskies from England, Scotland, Ireland and Wales.

And so The ONE was born – the first and only British whisky.

The Union may have been under threat, but The Lakes Distillery team was determined to create something that proved, alcoholically if not ideologically, that we truly were better together.

Alan recalls: "I realised right away that this was a great idea and would almost certainly be a success, not least because it had never been done before.

"From a practical point of view, we needed to be selling something from 'day one', not only to bring in some money to support the business but also to show that something was actually happening at the distillery and to get people talking about it."

Blends, however, were often much maligned and the team knew

WE ARE AT THE BEGINNING OF CHANGE IN WHISKY PRODUCTION, A CHANGE THAT IS INTERNATIONAL AND WILL CHALLENGE THE DOMINANCE OF SCOTLAND.

they had a tough job on their hands to change perceptions.

Paul Currie concedes: "Blends still have a poor reputation because people tend to think of them as the cheaper stuff on supermarket shelves.

"However, there's a real skill involved in blending and, at the top end of the market, blends can be very, very good indeed.

"Had we launched The ONE ten years ago, I think it would have struggled to gain acceptance but, thankfully, perceptions are beginning to change."

Since its launch, The ONE has certainly done its bit to raise the bar, winning a Silver Legend award at the prestigious International Wine and Spirit Competition (IWSC) in 2014, followed by another Silver Legend award in the Worldwide Whisky category of the

Hong Kong IWSC, aimed at the Asian market, followed by a Silver Outstanding in the 2015 IWSC.

This was no mean feat for a total newcomer to the blended whisky arena.

The annual HKIWSC awards are an industry-noted mark of quality and excellence, and provide the Asian market with the ultimate guide to purchasing wine and spirits which are sensitive to the Asian palate and cultural consumption patterns.

Products from almost 40 countries are entered, with only those of the highest quality receiving recognition.

Entries undergo intense scrutiny including double-blind tastings and technical analysis.

Paul Currie said of The ONE's success: "These awards set the benchmark for quality and the vast population of consumers in Asia eagerly anticipate the results each year."

With the likelihood of further accolades on the horizon, and upmarket outlets such as Harvey Nichols, Fortnum and Mason and Majestic Wines stocking it, The ONE has clearly carved out a niche.

So how did The Lakes Distillery team go about the business of creating the first ever British Isles blend?

Not for the first time, Dr Alan Rutherford's inside knowledge and contacts proved critical. As Chairman of Compass Box, a specialist Scotch whisky maker with a blending operation in Chiswick, London, he was able to call on the services of one of the world's most respected whisky makers, John Glaser.

Alan says: "Once we had John on board with myself and Paul, it really was just a case of trial and error.

"We knew what sort of blend we were aiming for – it had to be distinctive whilst at the same time easy-drinking and approachable."

Those unfamiliar with blended whiskies might be surprised to learn that most contain between 20 and 30 different malts. The reason for this, says Alan, is that there is "safety in numbers."

He explains: "Whiskies vary a little from cask to cask and from year to year, and sometimes distilleries go out of business or a particular whisky is no longer available.

WITH MOST
INDUSTRIES YOU
MAKE SOMETHING
TODAY AND YOU SELL
IT TOMORROW, BUT
THE WORLD OF
WHISKY IS NOT
LIKE THAT. YOU
HAVE TO KEEP
THE FAITH. YOU
HAVE TO DO
EVERYTHING
RIGHT AND
THEN STICK
IT OUT FOR
A LONG
TIME BEFORE
YOU HAVE
SOMETHING
REALLY
WORTHWHILE.

"If that happens, and you don't have many whiskies in your blend, you will have difficulty maintaining the consistency.

"But if you have 20-plus whiskies in your blend and you lose one, it's not so crucial. You can always find something similar to replace it."

What is vital, however, is to use good quality base blends as a starting point. The Lakes Distillery team deliberated long and hard before choosing some exceptional whiskies from Scotland.

From there it was a case of introducing other complementary whiskies to the mix to create the unique British Isles recipe.

Alan adds: "I think we have something very special with The ONE and it's no surprise to me that it has done so well.

"I'm actually a very big fan of blended whisky, in fact, I drink more blends than malts, which tends to surprise people.

"I happen to think they are more interesting and they're also lighter and more easy-going for everyday drinking.

"I often liken my appreciation for whisky to listening to music. You can enjoy a good solo performance, which is what you get from a malt, but what appeals to me most is a really great orchestra!"

Despite his experience and almost encyclopaedic knowledge of the industry, Alan has no truck with whisky snobs.

He says: "Don't let anyone tell you how you should be drinking your whisky – it's entirely down to individual taste.

"If you prefer to drown it in Coca Cola or some other mixer, that's fine, so long as it gives you enjoyment.

"Personally, I add only bottled still water. At least as much as there is whisky, and usually a touch more. And I also like a little ice.

"I never drink it neat because, in my view, 40% alcohol on the palate hides the character and flavour. But that's just my preference. Everyone is different.

"If you're not sure how you like it, I'd recommend you start by adding just a little water, then progressively add more until you find the flavour that most appeals to you.

"And, if after trying all of that you still prefer Coca Cola, then go ahead. There are no hard and fast rules!"

THE ONE

So many whiskies, so much choice.
The Lakes Distillery spirit was willing
and waiting. The skill lay in making
this bottle stand out from the rest.

A week may be a long time in politics, in whisky-naming it's a terrifyingly brief timescale.

When the original name and branding of The Lakes Distillery Whisky had to be abandoned at the last minute for legal reasons, the team was left with just a week to come up with a new concept for a presentation they were scheduled to make to potential investors.

They turned to creative design agency Hedley McEwan of Newcastle and gave them five days to find a solution. The clock was ticking.

THE ONE BRITISH
BLENDED WHISKY

THE
LAKES DISTILLERY
CUMBRIA

Product of the UK

Duncan McEwan says: "I don't think any of these things happen purely by inspiration, you've got to put a lot of work into it. I developed pillars of thought around what it could be and I was thinking of things like Britishness and an island nation and togetherness. I did loads of alternatives, about 18 altogether. But on the togetherness aspect, one idea stood out like a sore thumb because it was the only British whisky; that was to call it The ONE."

Not only did it encapsulate the whole brand but it lent itself perfectly to advertising, as alcohol advertising cannot promote excessive consumption. But this brand could be promoted under lines such as "Just have The ONE", or, "We only ever drink The ONE".

He was convinced that it would already be registered as a trade mark but, to his amazement, in the alcohol category, it wasn't.

His research revealed that despite the tweedy, old-fashioned image whisky had once had, it was now enjoying worldwide popularity with younger markets. Also, because The ONE was the first British whisky, it didn't have to follow the more rigorous conventions of Scotch and Irish designs and branding.

"I thought, hang on, we've got a blank sheet of paper here," says Duncan. "If it's going to appeal to the fastest growing market, that's the young, it can have a totally different feel from anything that's gone before. So I gave it a more kind of stripped back, simple, clean, fresh, sort of Scandinavian simplicity. Because we were stripping it back and being simple, we wouldn't have a label, we'd print straight onto the bottle and just give it a look, that wasn't like anything else, which we were legitimately able to, because it was the first, it was the one and only."

After that, the other spirits slotted neatly into the same branding concept. Gin, like The ONE, is three letters and vodka was easily abbreviated by stripping out the "ka" and putting it in the "D", giving it the same three letter form design.

"It made a lovely little family," says Duncan. "It just works so well as a little family of new brands and all have that nice, clean, fresh, new, youthful look about them."

ONE

THE

NE BRITISH
DED WHISKY

THE
DISTILLERY
CUMBRIA   40% alc /vol

TEAM

The best whisky needs more than the purest water, top quality barley, state-of-the-art equipment and the best casks money can buy. It needs truly gifted professionals adding the human touch.

December 17, 2017 will be a landmark day. It will mark three years since the first cask was filled, a day when our precious spirit officially becomes a single malt whisky, in this case, The Lakes Malt.

The expectation will be of 'a lightly peated drop of liquid gold with a delicate, floral aroma and sweet taste'.

Every chance the prediction will be right.

Dr Alan Rutherford and his team are confident they will have a winner on their hands.

By then, that near-perfect River Derwent water will have completed its journey, in distance, from its source high up in the hills of Upper Borrowdale at Sprinkling Tarn, and in time, from fermentation and distillation through to the all-important 1,095-day maturation.

Throughout this time, skilled craftsmen will have been monitoring the spirit's progress, their role every bit as essential as those precious three ingredients of barley, yeast and water.

Two key figures in this process are Master Distiller Chris Anderson and Distillery Manager John Drake, neither of whom could have ever foreseen the day when they would be making English whisky in the heart of the Lake District National Park.

The catalyst for bringing Chris on board was Dr Alan Rutherford,

L–R Rachel Palmer, Tracey Craft, Laura Simpson, Brian Jobling, Terry Laybourne, Gary Thornton, Paul Currie, Nigel Mills, Martin Stokoe, John Drake, Andy Beaton

Poppy Fisher, Business Development

Katie Read, Senior National Accounts Manager

Liz Parkes, Business Development Manager

Laura Simpson, Brand Manager

Dr Alan Rutherford

who had earlier been approached by Nigel Mills and Paul Currie to scrutinise the distillery's business plan due to his vast experience in the industry.

He recalls: "One of the main reasons I agreed to be on the board was that I was so impressed by Nigel and Paul's plan, it was one of the best I'd ever seen for a new distillery.

"They had taken a long-term view and it was obvious from the outset I was dealing with professionals. I also had this gut feeling that building a distillery in the Lake District was a great idea.

"I feel we are at the beginning of change in whisky production, a change that is international and will challenge the dominance of Scotland. So I believed there was a great future in English whisky and that it would be good to be involved in the early stages of this revolution.

"They point to the wine industry and the dominance, 30 years ago, of European countries such as France, Italy, Spain and Germany.

"Now their output has been surpassed by Australia, with other 'New World' producers also enjoying a sizeable market share. But if English whisky, and The Lakes Malt in particular, is to be taken seriously, it needs more than the purest water, top quality barley, state-of-the-art equipment and the best casks money can buy. It needs truly gifted professionals to make the most of these attributes. And that's where Chris and John come in.

Alan continues: "The principle of building a new distillery is great, but unless you have someone with hands-on experience who has mashed, worked stills and so on, it's very difficult to start from scratch."

Paul Currie had already found John Drake, a Cumbrian-born and bred man who was truly passionate about whisky, but had no hands-on experience.

What was needed was a bona fide expert who could take John under his wing and teach him everything he knew. That person was Chris Anderson. Chris comes from a long line of Scottish whisky distillers, beginning his career at Caol Ila. He also worked at Lagavulin before moving on to manage all of Dewar's distilleries, including Royal

Brackla, Aberfeldy, Craigellachie and Aultmore. He joined the industry in Scotland straight from school and has made distilling his life's work, and he takes exception to the notion that whisky contains just barley, yeast and water.

For Chris, there is a vital fourth ingredient that makes all the difference, people.

"The human touch is vital," he says. "And that is something I can honestly say is a factor here at The Lakes Distillery. Also, there have been no shortcuts taken and I would congratulate the board because they did not skimp with the costs, and the costs were huge. They were determined to have the best."

Chris was enjoying his retirement in Stirling after a 43-year career when he was persuaded to come to Cumbria by Alan, an old friend he had known since the 70s.

He recalls: "Alan phoned me and said 'I want you to go The Lakes Distillery and hold their hand because they're doing a little project'. That was over a year ago and I'm still here.

"I thought it would just be a case of getting it up and running production-wise, but it wasn't quite like that.

"There weren't exactly cows and sheep roaming around the building by the time I arrived, but they weren't long gone.

"I'm 67 now and people tell me I should be putting my feet up, but I'll be forever grateful to have been given the opportunity to be part of this. It can be frustrating at times, but it's also very exciting.

"The distillery's values, faith, hope, luck and love, are evident in everything the company does. But for me the most important of those values at the outset was faith.

"With most industries you make something today and you sell it tomorrow, but the world of whisky is not like that.

"So you have to keep the faith. You have to do everything right and then stick it out for a long time before you have something really worthwhile.

"That's true of the product and it's true of the company too. It's clear to me that the people who run this distillery are here for the long haul. They know it has a great future."

CONDENSERS

John Drake

Even though Chris has plans to retire, he expects to be involved with the distillery for the foreseeable future, and certainly until the hotly-anticipated The Lakes Malt makes its first appearance.

Stepping into his role when he does stand down for good will be John Drake, the current Distillery Manager. His route into the industry was far from conventional. A former civil servant and IT expert, John worked at the Sellafield nuclear reprocessing site near Seascale, Cumbria, before becoming a project manager for the British Cattle Moving Service, which operates a cattle tracing database, hardly the obvious credentials for whisky distillation.

However, he had one essential quality that Paul Currie liked, enthusiasm.

John says: "I have a holiday home on Islay and had visited most of the distilleries there. I wouldn't have called myself a connoisseur, but I did enjoy a wee dram.

"Then I read a story in the local paper about how Paul Currie was planning to set up a distillery in the Lake District.

"I live in Low Moresby, between Whitehaven and Workington, and I just thought it would be a fantastic industry to be part of so, half jokingly, I tried to persuade Paul to employ me as an IT project manager."

It was apparent to Paul, however, that whilst he had no need for an IT supremo, he would be in need of someone to run the day-to-day operation at the distillery - and that that someone might just be the exuberant, thirsty-for-knowledge whisky-lover in front of him.

John recalls: "I was in my late forties and had to go back to studying. I enrolled on the best course in the country, a Brewing and Distilling Post Graduate Diploma at Edinburgh's Heriot-Watt University.

"This was in 2010 and I was still employed by the government at the time. Then I took redundancy and continued my studies for another year. It was quite a leap of faith but my wife and family were incredibly supportive."

With Chris's help, John was able to spend time at some of Scotland's most prestigious distilleries including Aberfeldy and Aultmore, experiences he says proved invaluable.

"Chris is a legend in the industry, although he's far too modest to admit that himself," says John.

"But the truth is he has probably forgotten more about whisky production than I will ever know. And I realise how fortunate I am to have him as my mentor.

"I'm eternally grateful for everything he has done for me and I know that when he finishes working here it will be my job to ensure the high standards he has set are maintained."

John admits he could never have predicted the complete turnabout his life has taken since he became involved with The Lakes Distillery. He did not, he insists, have an epiphany or Eureka moment when he realised his future was in whisky; it was more a case of stumbling into it almost by accident.

"If I'd spent too much time thinking about it, I'd have probably seen too many negatives," he says.

"But at the time it didn't feel like I was risking a lot. And even though there may have been occasions early on when I wondered if all the plans were going to get off the ground, I had faith in the people at the top.

"But I can't claim this turn of events in my life was planned in any way, I've just had to strap myself in and go with the ride."

Going forward, John's role will be to shoulder more responsibility as the weeks and months progress and the day of reckoning dawns, when The Lakes Malt finally comes of age.

He is confident that Chris and Alan's dream of a light and delicate, sweet tasting malt will be achieved.

"I think what sets this industry apart from another chemical operation that, for example, makes soap powder or whatever, is that workers take a huge amount of pride in what they do.

"They understand they are making something for people's pleasure and enjoyment and that shows in their attention to detail."

It seems clear that a knowledge and love of whisky is not all Chris and John share, there's a philosophy too, an understanding that people are, indeed, the 'fourth ingredient' that can make the difference between a routine whisky and one that shines.

ANGELS'
SHARE

During its time in the barrel, about 2% of the spirit is lost through natural evaporation every year. And after 10 years, as much as 25% can be lost. This is known as 'the Angels' Share' and is one of the reasons older whiskies are more expensive: there is simply less in the cask to bottle.

SPIRIT

The alchemy of Cumbrian botanicals and the purest mountain water give The Lakes Gin and The Lakes Vodka a unique artisan taste which reflects the ethos of The Lakes Distillery. Unrivalled surroundings and provenance of ingredients are crucial to the spirits' success and they are already reaping industry awards. The newest additions to The Lakes Distillery family also have a high-speed ambassador.

CHEMMY

Tucked away in the far corner of the distillery, Chemmy is somewhat dwarfed by big sister stills, Susan and Rachel. But appearances can be deceptive and this little pot still works every bit as hard as her siblings to create the spirit that will become The Lakes Gin and The Lakes Vodka.

Unlike Susan and Rachel, she has no family connection to business partners Nigel Mills or Paul Currie, but is named after Chemmy Alcott, Britain's number one female alpine skier.

Nigel says: "Chemmy said in an interview that what she really enjoyed after a day's skiing in the mountains was a good gin and tonic, so we rang her and asked if she would be interested in teaming up with the distillery and she was very enthusiastic about the project, we think she's a brilliant brand ambassador."

Chemmy's quality on the slopes made her Britain's top performer at the 2014 Winter Olympics in Sochi, Russia. And the performance of her pot still namesake at The Lakes Distillery is equally impressive, turning out award-winning gin and vodka that stands head and shoulders above the plethora of mass market spirits available.

In 2014, The Lakes Gin won a Silver Medal at the International Spirits Challenge, ahead of popular brand Hendrick's, which received Bronze, and The Lakes Vodka won a Bronze Medal in its category. The gin also won Silver at a separate competition targeted specifically for the Asian market, proving its global appeal.

Paul Currie believes the importance of these awards cannot be overstated.

"For a new brand, these accolades are absolutely crucial, and people in the trade understand that," he says.

"For me to be able to approach someone and be in a position to say 'try our amazing new gin, voted better than Hendrick's and here's the proof', well, that can really open doors.

"It's the sort of thing that gives you credibility among those who haven't heard of you – an immediate stamp of approval – so it's very important."

THE LAKES

GIN

GO

The only gin distilled in
The Lake District

Whilst whisky distillation will always be at the heart of the operation, Nigel and Paul planned from the outset to make gin and vodka too. With The Lakes Malt three years from bottling, they felt it was important to have not only an alternative revenue stream, but also something other than The ONE to cater for non-whisky drinkers. And they were keen for the distillery to be producing something unique and branded from day one.

With the phenomenal rise of artisan distilleries over the past decade, gin and vodka ticked all the boxes.

The craft gin revolution in particular has spread beyond its traditional London heartland to permeate far flung corners of the UK. The growth of small, traditional distillers has fuelled a renewed interest in this quintessentially English tipple which, in turn, has led to dedicated gin bars opening in many city centres.

"WITH OUR GIN, HOWEVER, WE'RE TURNING BACK THE CLOCK HUNDREDS OF YEARS. OUR SMALL, TRADITIONAL POT STILL HAS A CAPACITY OF JUST 1,000 LITRES, AND THAT'S THE WAY STILLS WERE IN THE 1700S"

And so, once again, the distillery team was faced with the challenge of producing something that stood out from the crowd – something capable of stealing the thunder of established brands at prestigious competitions. For The Lakes Gin, there are three key elements that give it an all-important edge, starting with what is arguably the distillery's greatest asset – that near-perfect River Derwent water.

"Generally the big gin producers are using tap water from London, whereas our water is near perfect, and that really does make a difference," explains Paul.

"Most of the gin sold in the UK is made on an industrial scale by three big distilleries in England. With our gin, however, we're turning back the clock hundreds of years. Our small, traditional pot still has a capacity of just 1,000 litres, and that's the way stills were in the 1700s.

"Bigger operations use something called a column still which is a much faster process, so their spirit doesn't get as much copper contact as ours does, and that makes quite a difference to the end product too; it really is a case of mass production against the artisan, slow approach we take. And finally, the third factor, and probably the biggest, is the botanical mix we have come up with."

Paul and his team called on the services of Rob Dorsett, of Midlands-based Alcohols Ltd, who is widely recognised as one of the world's leading experts on gin production. Over several weeks of trial and error, when ingredients such as grapefruit were considered and then ditched for being too overpowering, they finally arrived at what has been described as a "complex and vibrant" gin with fresh, citrus flavours and a fruity and floral aroma. And they are proud that, of the 14 ingredients that make up the botanical mix, six have been sourced from Cumbria, including some of the all-important juniper berries. All gin has a predominantly juniper flavour – the word 'gin' is derived from the Dutch word for juniper, jenever – but into that mix are added other key ingredients, such as coriander, cinnamon and liquorice.

"We have those ingredients in our gin, but we also have local junipers, along with Cumbrian meadowsweet, heather, hawthorn, bilberry and mint," says Paul.

"So this is the first gin that has ever included these six botanicals from Cumbria, and that helps give it its unique and distinctive flavour.

"In fact, it tastes so amazing that it doesn't need a mixer or any other embellishments like lemon or cucumber. Our advice is to chill it down in the freezer for an hour, then pour it over ice and drink it neat.

"But if you are partial to a gin and tonic, we suggest a ratio of 1:1... with no added fruit!"

THE
LAKES DISTILLERY
CUMBRIA

McMillan
www.mcmillanltd.co.uk

CHEMMY

For the spirit to become gin, it is steeped overnight in the botanicals so that the full flavour and character of the ingredients is absorbed – a world away from the mass market approach which, in the worst cases, involves the use of artificial flavours.

Paul adds: "All told, with the steeping process and distillation, our gin takes around 17 hours to make, compared with around an hour or two for many popular brands.

"IN OUR GIN WE ALSO HAVE LOCAL JUNIPERS, ALONG WITH CUMBRIAN MEADOWSWEET, HEATHER, HAWTHORN, BILBERRY AND MINT SO THIS IS THE FIRST GIN THAT HAS EVER INCLUDED THESE SIX BOTANICALS FROM CUMBRIA, AND THAT HELPS GIVE IT ITS UNIQUE AND DISTINCTIVE FLAVOUR"

"All these factors in isolation have an effect, but when you put them together, the water, the small pot still, the amazing botanical mix and the time we take to do the job properly, it all contributes to a taste that has won us critical acclaim."

The distillery is heavily involved in the preservation of the local environment and, as such, sponsors the Cumbria Wildlife Trust, which collects juniper berries on its behalf. The trust is the guardian of this important natural resource, replenishing stocks and protecting established plants from sheep, which like to feast on them.

Paul says: "The trust does excellent work in protecting the region's juniper, and there's certainly a lot more of it about now than there was five or ten years ago.

"And that's great news for us because Cumbrian juniper has a bit more character to it than most juniper you get in gin, which tends to come from the Balkan states or Greece."

A renewed interest in vodka has also been triggered by the artisan renaissance. And with the majority (54%) of white spirit drinkers declaring it their preferred tipple, it would have been foolish for The Lakes Distillery to ignore this. Unlike gin, however, pure vodka is not flavoured as such, making it even more difficult for distillers to differentiate their products. So where do you begin?

Paul says: "A lot of vodka – even more so than gin – is made on a massive, industrial scale. And often that means no one has a clue about its origins – it's just basic alcohol.

"But, as with our gin, we have the benefit of an amazing water source and our marvellous little pot still, so the process we use gives the vodka a real flavour.

"We triple distil our vodka for greater purity, producing a taste of outstanding character and complexity.

"We're confident that if you tried it alongside many of the standard brands people are familiar with, you would certainly be able to tell the difference."

Clearly, that confidence is reflected in The Lakes Vodka's recent silver medal at the IWSC, added to a bronze won at the International Spirit Challenge.

The vodka also has its own unique look. Working in association with famed tea and alcohol artist Carne Griffiths, the distillery has created an unlikely partnership, blending art and vodka as one. Seen throughout The Lakes Vodka brand is work produced by Carne for exclusive use to become what the distillery team calls 'The Art of Vodka.'

Meanwhile, after her success in Sochi, The Lakes Gin brand ambassador Chemmy Alcott announced her retirement from competitive skiing.

It seems clear, however, that with two award-winning spirits to produce, her namesake at the distillery will be kept busy for some time to come.

LAKES GIN TASTING NOTES
Big, clear fresh citrus, fruity and
floral. Complex and vibrant.

LAKES VODKA TASTING NOTES
Rich aroma with a hint of wheat,
ultra-smooth and silky, full of character.

THE ART OF VODKA

The Lakes Distillery team was inspired by the work of the famed tea and alcohol artist Carne Griffiths who has added some artistic drama to their spirit.

Carne will create a limited edition print of the distillery for the Connoisseurs club members which will eventually be available to buy in the distillery shop.

His works actually use alcohol within the liquids he paints with and his style draws on the natural ingredients which go into The Lakes Distillery gin and vodka.

He works with calligraphy inks, graphite and liquids, such as tea, whisky and vodka to create soft, romantic drawings which in the case of The Lakes Distillery, reflect the natural ingredients and surroundings which inspire them.

He describes why he began working with drinkable liquids: "I had always worked with calligraphy ink and water. It was a glass of brandy that led to the first splash of drinkables on the page.

"Alcohol has a curious effect on ink, taking the colour deep into the paper very quickly - it behaves very differently to water and gives permanence to some inks."

His works look almost ethereal and dreamy with their focus the link between natural environment and the growing living elements which take their place in the spirits that are created.

Soft grasses, herbs and berries meet with languid waters and gentle landscape for paintings which show the richness of nature and its link to an artisan product.

Griffiths' paintings bring a different sense of originality to The Lakes Distillery's products and the link with the natural environment.

THE ARTIST ACTUALLY USES ALCOHOL WITHIN THE LIQUIDS HE PAINTS WITH AND HIS STYLE DRAWS ON THE NATURAL INGREDIENTS WHICH GO INTO THE LAKES DISTILLERY GIN AND VODKA

SUSTAIN

From the beginning, the Lakes Distillery
has immersed itself in the community that
surrounds it. The very word whisky is
derived from the Gaelic uisge beatha,
meaning water of life. The Lakes Distillery
embraces its duty to nurture and protect
that life.

I t is hardly surprising that The Lakes Distillery should be so proud of its environment and heritage and be determined to protect and preserve it.

The result is that The Lakes Distillery is one of the most environmentally friendly in the world.

Biomass boilers, burning fuel from sustainable sources, are used for all heating and hot water on the site; the draff, or barley waste from the whisky production, is fed to local cattle; The Lakes Distillery has its own on-site sewerage plant and recycled water is used for cooling the plant.

The site is also located on the main bus route between Keswick and Cockermouth so that staff and visitors can minimise their use of cars. The Lakes Distillery seeks not only to sustain the natural life around it but also the community among which it operates.

A percentage of proceeds from its main products go to support three Lakeland charities: The ONE supports Great North Ambulance; The Lakes Gin supports Cumbria Wildlife Trust, who are the guardians of juniper trees in Cumbria, the key ingredient of The Lakes Gin; and the The Lakes Vodka contributes to Fix the Fells, who help maintain footpaths and repair erosion damage.

The Lakes Distillery has created more than 50 jobs in North West Cumbria and it strives to be a thoroughly Cumbrian operation, built by Cumbrians and, in renovating it, where materials could not be recycled, they were replaced from within the National Park.

Founder Nigel Mills says: "We have invested a lot of time and money in this area and we are very fond of it. In The Lakes Distillery which is a tourist destination as well as a manufacturing operation, I think we have created something very special which will help boost the local economy, not least in the fact that we have created 50 jobs.

"We bought the Trout Hotel in 1989 and it was the people of Cumbria and the local builders and joiners and electricians that have done all the work that helped develop this business.

"When we bought the hotel it was 23 bedrooms and £600,000 turnover, it's now 49 bedrooms, two bars, three different food

and beverage operations, employs 75 people and turns over £3.1m.

The Lakes Distillery is an extension of the growth and development of Cumbrian business that we have carried out at the Trout Hotel which creates job and career opportunity."

Coincidentally, at around the time the Lakes Distillery was opening, the North West Cumbria tourism body was being wound up due to a lack of funding. But the marketing undertaken by the Lakes Distillery helped to keep tourism for the area on the map.

Little wonder then that The Lakes Distillery has been welcomed by the community.

"It has been incredibly well received by the locals," says Nigel. "They are the ones who have supported us. The tourists come en masse between April and October and for the remaining five months you have only got the local market.

"It was great to open in December when the tourists weren't around because it gave the locals the opportunity to adopt it as their own and they certainly have. We have been taken aback by their support and their enthusiasm for the project and the way they helped promote it.

"We've had amazing support from the hoteliers, the bed and breakfast operators, the caravan parks and the local traders because they are delighted to see somebody put this sort of commitment and investment into this part of the region."

As a place the Lake District is full of life, both in its beautiful natural environment and in its warm and welcoming communities.

From the beginning, The Lakes Distillery has immersed itself in that life and made itself a part of it. The very word whisky is derived from the Gaelic uisge beatha which means water of life. The Lakes Distillery's spirits come from the life of the Lakes and it embraces its duty to nurture and protect that life.

TASTE

The best of Cumbrian produce finds its way to the Bistro at the Distillery with inspired ingredients, not least the odd drop of gin, vodka and whisky from stills on-site.

With its elegant, unfussy décor, clean lines and impressive arched windows affording views into a stylish courtyard, it's easy to see why the Bistro at the Distillery is such a hit with visitors.

Add to the mix excellent service, stir in some delicious food, beautifully presented, and you have an offering every bit as potent as the slowly maturing malt on site.

On the menu the philosophy is to reflect as much as possible the bistro's unique location, both in terms of the distillery itself and the wider environment.

So it's no surprise to find whisky-tinged desserts and truffles or meat served with a sauce made from the same locally-sourced juniper that flavours The Lakes Gin. Or that, whenever possible, meat and seasonal vegetables are locally sourced too.

The man behind the food is restaurateur Terry Laybourne, a man with an impeccable pedigree. He was the first chef to bring a Michelin Star to North East England in 1992, an accolade he and his 21 Queen Street restaurant held for nine years before he switched focus to develop a string of more casual, bistro-style eateries.

As founder of the 21 Hospitality Group, his culinary arsenal includes Café 21, Caffé Vivo, Broad Chare and Café 21 at Fenwick's department store in Newcastle, as well as Bistro 21 in Durham.

Once described as the "uncrowned king of Newcastle" by celebrity

chef Marco Pierre White, Terry's influence is such that, in 1999, he received an MBE for his contribution to the restaurant industry and tourism.

He says: "I don't obsess about the local thing; at the end of the day I want the very best produce for the restaurant. If I can get that locally, great. If not, I'll look further afield.

"In a way, that sums up my philosophy when it comes to food. I'm far more interested in product than technique.

"The guy who rears the pig and then cures the meat to produce a wonderful leg of ham, he's the artist.

"If he does his job well, all I have to do is put a nice sharp knife through it.

"Obviously there is expertise involved in deciding how I present the ham and what I serve it with, but that doesn't make me an artist because all I have done is find the best man who cures the best meat."

More than anything else, it is this uncompromising commitment to finding the very best produce and serving it with skill and panache that has spread the word about the bistro.

"West Cumbria is a relatively small community and in small communities news travels fast, so we're absolutely thrilled that our restaurant has been so warmly received and is doing so well. It's a testament to the hard work and commitment of everyone involved.

"My mission was to create a restaurant that could stand on its own two feet, a restaurant that's good enough to attract customers irrespective of who is behind it or where it is. In that respect, the fact that it is attached to a distillery is almost academic. It's a bonus, of course, but people have got to want to come here regardless of that."

And come they have. Despite Terry's reservations about the timing of the 70-seater bistro's opening on December 15, 2014, business was brisk from day one and has never let up.

"In a way, the timing was tricky," he recalls. "People plan for Christmas, so we were too late for the natural uplift restaurants usually get and we had the cold, bleak nights of January and February stretching out in front of us.

"Having said that, I need not have worried as the local people

were fully behind us and the place was buzzing from day one. As a restaurateur, after all the months of meticulous planning, it was hugely gratifying and reassuring to witness the bistro take off and radiate such a warmth and conviviality as customers embraced the venture."

Terry's involvement in the project is partly down to his longstanding friendship with the distillery's entrepreneurial chairman Nigel Mills, and partly a result of his own innate curiosity and inability to resist a challenge.

He admits: "At the end of the day I got sucked into this for the same reasons Nigel, Paul and everyone else involved did; there was more than a touch of romance about the project. It has always felt like something really special.

"Nigel has very high aspirations. From the start he was using phrases like 'world class' within weeks and that brought with it a certain amount of pressure I guess."

Terry had met Nigel at an Entrepreneurs' Forum debate at which Nigel, the chairman, would be asking Terry questions. The two got together to "get our stories straight" and the conversation turned to other matters, including Nigel's distillery project, England's biggest whisky distillery in the heart of the Lake District National Park.

Terry recalls: "I was excited by it straight away. I thought that's an interesting prospect, so when Nigel said he was looking for investors something chimed with me immediately."

Having been bowled over by Nigel's enthusiasm and his grand plans

for a 'world class' eatery in the tiny village of Setmurthy, population 93, Terry adds: "I asked Nigel what his vision was for the restaurant and he said it was to create a Cumbrian business for Cumbrian people staffed by Cumbrians using Cumbrian produce.

"I made it my mission to find the right people to give the restaurant an identity and a heart and soul of its own.

"I didn't want to recreate a carbon copy of one of my other restaurants, that wouldn't have been interesting at all. There was no point in just helicoptering something in from Newcastle and dropping it into the Lake District, the Bistro at the Distillery had to have its own personality that would evolve organically."

He discovered an "exceptional" manager in Rachel Palmer and his "gem" of a head chef is the Raymond Blanc-trained Andrew Beaton, ambitious and eager to make his mark after spending seven years at a respected restaurant in Windermere.

Terry says: "My role now is a supportive one, I don't want the limelight. It's really important that the line is led by the head chef and manager.

"We got off to a great start and it has just continued, but we will never rest on our laurels. The menu will remain tight and focused, and will change with the seasons and be spontaneous on occasions.

"And it will constantly evolve and mature over the coming years... just like the whisky next door!"

ROASTED CUMBRIAN VENISON WITH GIN AND JUNIPER SAUCE SERVES 4

MARINADE

65g	Carrot, peeled and finely sliced
65g	Onion, peeled and finely sliced
15g	Celery, finely sliced
10g	Butter
250ml	Red wine
25ml	Red wine vinegar
160ml	Water
1	Small bouquet garni
1	Rosemary sprig
1	Clove

Sweat the vegetables in butter without colouring.
Add the remaining ingredients and bring to a boil, reduce the heat and simmer for 20 minutes.
Remove from the heat and allow to cool fully

VENISON

700g Roe deer saddle – fully trimmed

Place the venison into a deep dish and pour the marinade over. Cover with a piece of oiled greaseproof paper and refrigerate for 2 days, turning from time to time.
Remove the venison from the marinade and pat dry on kitchen paper.
Strain the marinade into a small saucepan.

GIN AND JUNIPER SAUCE

	The strained marinade (as before)
150ml	Veal stock (or brown chicken stock)
1tsp	Juniper berries (crushed slightly)
1tbls	The Lakes Gin
10g	Unsalted butter

Bring the marinade to a boil and skim carefully.
Add the veal stock and juniper berries, simmer to reduce by half.
Add the gin and swirl in the unsalted butter.
Check the seasoning and finish with a good grind of white pepper.

TO FINISH

Season the venison with salt and a generous amount of pepper.
Heat the oil in a heavy frying pan or roasting tray and add the venison, followed by the butter.
Transfer to the pre-heated oven for 4-5 minutes and cook to medium rare (54°C core temperature).
Remove the meat and rest in a warm place, loosely covered with foil for 5 – 10 minutes before carving into generous slices.
Serve coated with the gin and juniper sauce
Accompany with seasonal fruits and vegetables.

WHISKY MARMALADE
PUDDING SERVES 4

PUDDING

100g	Caster sugar
2	Medium eggs
110g	Unsalted butter (softened)
100g	Self raising flour
1tsp	Baking powder
1/4tsp	Finely-grated orange rind
280g	Whisky marmalade
	Soft butter and flour for moulds

Warm the sugar on a sheet of greaseproof paper in a low oven.

Whisk eggs until white then shower in the warm sugar and continue whisking until cool.

Whisk in the soft butter.

Sift the self raising flour and baking powder together and then fold into the mixture.

Fold in the grated zests.

Brush four individual pudding moulds with softened butter then dust with flour, discarding excess flour.

Divide the marmalade between the moulds then top with the sponge mixture (to around ¾ full)

Cover loosely with buttered tin foil and steam for 50 minutes.

WHISKY MARMALADE

1 x 340g jar	Best quality Seville orange marmalade
1½ tbls	The ONE whisky

Gently warm the marmalade in a microwave
Stir in The ONE.

TO SERVE

Remaining whisky marmalade, warmed
400ml Crème Anglaise (or custard).

Turn out the hot puddings into warm bowls and spoon the remaining whisky marmalade over.

Froth up the Crème Anglaise with a hand blender and spoon a generous quantity over and around the pudding.

The puddings can be made well in advance and heated gently in a microwave.

CHOCOLATE TRUFFLES

220g	UHT whipping cream
940g	Milk chocolate couverture
20g	Unsalted butter
50ml	The ONE Whisky
	Creative powder (available from cake decorating retailers)

Bring the cream to a boil.

Pour half of the cream over 440g of chocolate and allow to stand for a few minutes.

Add the remaining cream and mix with a spatula until smooth.

Add the whisky and mix again.

Check the temperature and adjust to 32°C before mixing in the butter. Transfer to a clean container, cover and refrigerate overnight.

Next day, cut the truffles using a melon baller and lay them on to greaseproof paper – return to the fridge.

Gently melt the remaining chocolate in a microwave on defrost setting, stirring from time to time. Ensure the temperature doesn't exceed 35°C.

Roll each ball by hand, coating with the melted chocolate. Transfer to greaseproof paper to set at room temperature. Do not refrigerate until the chocolate is fully set.

Once set, dip a dry pastry brush into creative powder and dust the truffles gently to give a golden shimmer.

Serve in a whisky tumbler or package in a little rolled acetate tied with ribbon.

COCKTAIL RECIPES

THE CHEMMY

GLASS/ICE
Martini glass
Chilled

INGREDIENTS
2 x shots The Lakes Gin
1 x shot freshly squeezed grapefruit juice
1/2 x shot Martini extra dry
Barspoon sugar syrup

METHOD/STRAIN
Shake over ice
Double strain

GARNISH
Grapefruit twist

WHISKY SOUR

GLASS/ICE
Rocks glass
Crushed ice

INGREDIENTS
2 x shots The ONE
1 x shot lemon juice
1/2 x shot sugar syrup
3 dashes Angostura bitters
1/2 shot egg white (optional)

METHOD/STRAIN
Dry shake all ingredients (if using egg)
Shake again with ice
Strain into glass
Top with crushed ice

GARNISH
Lemon and cherry flag
2 clear sip straws

ELDERFLOWER MARTINI

GLASS/ICE
Martini glass
Chilled

INGREDIENTS
2 x shots The Lakes Vodka
1 x shot St Germain
1 x shot lemon juice
1/2 x shot sugar syrup

METHOD/STRAIN
Shake over ice
Double strain

GARNISH
3 elderflower gooseberries on prism

BOARDROOM

While the whisky sleeps
The Lakes Distillery's grand
Boardroom provides a stunning
location to celebrate the essence
of the project.

The dramatic vaulted Boardroom has windows and mirrors overlooking the cellars and visitors are surrounded by the sense of place and the drama of the distillery process.

The Boardroom is where members of the Connoisseurs' Club and Founders' Club will gather to toast the arrival of the first Lakes Distillery Malt.

Connoisseurs' Club members will own their own cask, each estimated to contain more than 100 bottles. On the historic first day they will be invited to fill their own Connoisseur's Cask and see it stored in the distillery warehouse overlooked by the Boardroom. That Connoisseur's Cask will forever bear their name.

The Boardroom will be a place for literally gathering in the spirit of The Lakes Distillery. A place to raise a glass to

formal dining, corporate hospitality and celebrations such as weddings, birthdays and anniversaries.

As with the rest of The Lakes Distillery, quality and attention to detail have been the key to making the Boardroom a unique place.

Handwoven carpets in a design that reflects the flow of the waters which supply the distillery.

Hand-crafted lights are made from amber glass which casts a glow redolent of the spirit that lies within the casks of sleeping spirit that can be seen through the windows in the Boardroom.

The huge table that forms the centrepiece of the Boardroom is of course made from oak, handcrafted by Cumbrian craftsmen.

The Boardroom is the place that pays homage to The Lakes Distillery's final product, as near as it gets to being the spirit in the cask.

SHOP &
SAMPLE

The Tasting Room at The Lakes Distillery is where the distillery tour ends. The place where, appetites whetted, visitors can taste the whisky, gin or vodka produced on site.

T he Tasting Room is the perfect place to linger, backed by a beautiful etched glass mural depicting the journey of the water that is used to make The Lakes Distillery spirits, from Sprinkling Tarn to the sea.

By this point, visitors will have immersed themselves in the romantic story and surroundings of The Lakes Distillery and can wander around the shop which is a showcase for The Lakes Distillery products.

It is a beautiful and relaxing retail experience where much thought has gone into the design and fitting of the area.

Craftsmen-built bespoke oak fittings are a stylish backdrop for The Lakes Distillery whisky, gin and vodka and accessories such as decanters and crystal glasses in contemporary and traditional designs.

The shop works with local craftsmen and suppliers to showcase products from, among others, Chapman's Bags, Maddi Alexander toiletries and Cumbrian Crystal. A number of products have been exclusively designed for The Lakes Distillery to reflect the Cumbrian heritage and story.

A ROYAL
TOAST

A royal seal of approval was the perfect
toast to the success of The Lakes
Distillery as Her Royal Highness,
The Princess Royal officially opened
the distillery and visitor centre.

Her visit marked The Lake Distillery's position as the newest visitor attraction in Cumbria and England's premier whisky distillery.

Founder and managing director of The Lakes Distillery, Paul Currie, welcomed her Royal Highness The Princess Royal to the distillery's picturesque setting overlooking Bassenthwaite Lake and gave her a tour of the £7m development. Her Royal Highness visited the stillroom where The Lakes Vodka, The Lakes Gin and The Lakes Malt are produced on-site, and the Bistro at the Lakes Distillery before unveiling a plaque in the distillery courtyard which marks its official opening.

Following the tour, Paul and chairman of the board, Nigel Mills, presented Her Royal Highness with a sherry cask of The Lakes Malt to commemorate her visit to The Lakes Distillery.

Paul said: "It was an incredible honour to have Her Royal Highness, The Princess Royal officially open The Lakes Distillery and all of us will remember it for years to come. As the only distillery in Cumbria, we are very proud of our team and our facilities which are already producing award-winning spirits. It was a pleasure to be able to present the fruit of our hard work to such a prestigious guest.

"Her Royal Highness' visit marks the start of our first summer season open to the public. We expect to attract 100,000 guests of all ages to the distillery each year, who will be able to follow the same tour as Her Royal Highness, and we hope they enjoy their visit just as much."

"I HOPE LOTS MORE PEOPLE GET TO SEE THE DISTILLERY AND THE WONDERFUL BENEFITS IT HAS HERE, FROM THE LOCAL WATER AND PERFECT ENVIRONMENT TO LOVELY BISTRO. IT IS ESPECIALLY LOVELY TO SEE AN OLD AGRICULTURAL BUILDING BEING RESTORED AND PUT TO GOOD USE. I'M LOOKING FORWARD TO COMING BACK."

PEOPLE

It's true that whisky is made with just three ingredients but it takes a special blend of people to make that magic happen. The team at The Lakes Distillery perfectly embodies the values of Faith, Hope, Luck and Love that run through this unique business.

DIRECTORS

Brian Jobling • Gary Thornton • Martin Stokoe
Nigel Mills • Paul Currie

NON-EXECUTIVE DIRECTORS

Mark Haigh • Philip Upton • David Mutch
Gillian Bolam • Alan Rutherford • Moray Martin
Laurance Laybourne • Phil Morris • Stewart Smith

GOSFORTH TEAM
L-R: Ash Westgate, Laura Richards, Amanda Whitlie, Nigel Mills,
Tracey Craft, Laura Simpson, Martin Stokoe, Joanne Brown, Mike
Hodgson, Helen Marshall

PRODUCTION TEAM

L-R: John Drake, Liam Jackson, Richard Birkett, Ronnie Smith

BISTRO TEAM

L-R: Kirsty Archer , Rachel Palmer, Suzi Atkinson, Jonny Kemp (seated),
Jordan Marshall, Tom Williamson, Jon Atkins, Danielle Leonard
(seated), Joanne Quinlan, Kate Gatford.

Not pictured: Terry Laybourne - Consultant, Eloise Eddington,
Callum Taylor, Emma Wilson, Chantelle Wilson, Georgia Horsley,
Emma Dawes, Charles Clarkson

KITCHEN TEAM
L-R: David Ditchburn, Gavin Moore, Andy Beaton, Jacob Pattinson,
Alex Sim, James McManus, Anna Czerwinska.

Not pictured: Danny Parsons, Robert Don, Josh Danson,
Dylan Rickerby

TOURS & RETAIL TEAM

L-R: Sue Wilkinson, Brian Hill, Sarah Scott, Esme Brame,
Andrew Dubieniec, Amanda Durkin

Not pictured: Simon Gray, Michael Palmer, Liz Parkes, Poppy
Fisher, Katie Read, Lou Crowther

A TOAST TO
THE FUTURE

The essence of The Lakes Distillery and Lakes Distillery brands is one of beauty, honesty and a heartfelt sense of place.

Though the Distillery is new, we have worked hard to create a feeling of heritage, both of the Lake District and the art of whisky making itself. That said, our vision is to look forwards, not back.

We have absorbed every drop of knowledge that is of value, yet applied the experience and flair of our uniquely talented team to break new ground, to push the boundaries and breathe fresh life into this ancient craft.

Being a new English distillery means we have no 'language' or 'look' we have to follow, no pseudo 'Celtic creed' which we need to evoke. We have in fact a blank canvas on which we can write our own history and tell our own story. Our brands therefore have the ability to present our products in a way that is fresh, contemporary and very different. The strength of our brands, the quality of our products and our ability to break new ground is what makes The Lakes Distillery so energetic and full of promise.

Nigel Mills
Chairman, The Lakes Distillery

THE LAKE DISTRICT'S NEWEST VISITOR ATTRACTION

ENGLAND'S PREMIER WHISKY DISTILLERY

THE LAKES DISTILLERY
CUMBRIA

There's something for all the family at The Lakes Distillery: a fascinating distillery tour, shop with our very own award winning whisky, gin and vodka, fantastic 'Bistro at the Distillery' and our friendly family of alpacas!

Tours run from 11am – 6pm daily. To book a tour call us on 017687 88857

www.lakesdistillery.com   The Lakes Distillery, Setmurthy, Bassenthwaite Lake, Cumbria CA13 9SJ

ROLL CALL

A project on the scale of The Lakes Distillery demands the efforts of a huge team of people working together. Meeting tight deadlines is one thing but doing so while maintaining the ultimate quality and attention to detail is quite another. We thank the people who have played their part in the creation of this unique distillery and visitor attraction. All should be justifiably proud.

CREATIVE

BluMilk • Geoff Hodgson • Creative

Brian Sherwin Photography • Brain Sherwin • Photography

Carne Griffiths Artist • Carne Griffiths • Artist

Damian Kane Photography • Damian Kane • Photography

Grasp • Brian Jobling • Web Design

Hedley McEwan • Dave Hampton, Duncan McEwan & Tom Hedley • Brand Design & Development

KG Photography • Kevin Gibson • Photographer for the book

Penny Lane Film Production • Penny Lane • TV & Radio Production Company

Re: Production • Steve Hunneysett • Film Production

Websand • Saul Gowens • Email Marketing

Wombat Creative • Fraser Hannah • Web Design

PRINT & PACKAGING

Bigger Scene • Adam Burrell • Large Format Print & Exhibitions

BLP • Cameron Butler, Kevin Scott • Print, Packaging & Direct Mail

Elanders • Matt Swift, Sean Mattimore, Chris Hewitt • Business & Commercial Packaging

Factory Framing • John & Susan Mostyn • Picture Framing

Radecal Signs • Nikko Liadopoulos • Signs & Graphics

Smurfitt Kappa • Nick Bridge, Helen Baird • Paper Based Packaging

MEDIA & PR

CN Group • Publishing

One Little Bird • Niki Hewitson • PR

OPR • Emma Campbell, Kari Owers, Caroline Cockburn • PR

Remember Media • Chris March, Kathryn Armstrong • Publishing Company

Tyson Hi Fi

BUILDING AND CONSTRUCTION

Architects Plus Limited • David Armstrong, David Blair • Architects

ROLL CALL

Aspire • Nigel Begg • Telecommunications
Enlighten

Bruce Armstrong-Payne • Planning Consultant

GMG Associates • Geoff Chatterley
• Quantity Surveyor

Grosvenor Wilton • Carpet Manufacturers

Honister Slate Mine • Michelle Blignault
• Slate Providers

John Whitfield • John Whitfield • Joinery

Lambert-Gill • John Parkinson - MD,
Jonty Kendall - Foreman Gary Dalgleish
• Builders

Metal Work Solutions

Pattinson Consultants • David Pattinson
• M&E Consultants

Peter Johnson & Co • Peter Johnson • Metal Work
& Railings

Peter Sibson Builder • Peter Sibson
• Independent Builder

Tweddell & Slater • Ted Slater • Structural Engineers

West End Cabinets & Joinery • David Saul
• Joinery Manufacturer

Zinc Counters • Duncan Grimmond • Zinc Counters

SCULPTURE

Adaptahaus • Alan Dawson • Metal Work (Gates)

Map Sculpture • Chris Scammell • Landscape Sculpture

INTERIOR DESIGN

Abercrombies Jesmond • Chris Stell, John Ord
• Interior Designer

DISTILLERY & PRODUCTION

Cochrans • Brian Peat, Tom Owens

CTS Process • Aleem Syed, David Rowe
• Dry Material Processing

EDA • Colin Hughes • Electrical Engineers

H & A Prestige • Linda Vass, Jo Fernandez

Holme Dodsworth Metals Limited • David Mutch

J L Rodriguez Toneleria • Maria Jose Rodriguez
Sherry Cask Suppliers

John M Bowler CEng MIMechE MIBD • Brewing
• Engineering Consultant

McMillans • David Allan • Engineering/Coppersmiths

Muntons • Pete Robson • Malt Suppliers

Musk Engineering • Engineering

Peter Laws • Brewing Consultant

ProControl Automation • Neil Phillips • Automation
Systems Programming

Speyside Cooperage • Willie Taylor,
Andrew Russell

191

ROLL CALL

FINANCE & GRANTS

Britain's Energy Coast

Graham Robinson • Royal Bank of Scotland

Manufacturing Advisory Service

Regional Growth Fund

Shareholders

Tier One Capital • Ian McElroy,
Stephen Black • Independent
Wealth Management

UKTI

LAWYERS

Bell Park Kerridge • Elizabeth Atkinson • Law Firm

Square One Law LLP • Ian Gilthorpe • Law Firm

Watson Burton LLP • Duncan Reid • Law Firm

CORPORATE PARTNERS

21 Hospitality Group

Architects Plus UK Limited • Architects

Brian Reay Taxis • Brian Reay

Entrepreneurs Forum • Gillian Marshall

Hedley McEwan • Brand Design & Development

Lake District National Park Authority

Lambert-Gill • Builders

Landowners • Keith & Julia Fisher

OPR • PR

Square One Law • Law Firm

Todd & Cue Ltd • Chris Scott • Insurance

Trout Hotels Cumbria Ltd • Sue Eccles

Public funding support came from Britain's Energy Coast and the Regional Growth Fund, as well as the Manufacturing Advisory Service and UKTI.